C000185805

Barley Barley

Also by Barrie Wade
Conkers

Barley Barley

Poems by Barrie Wade

Illustrated by Irene Wise

Oxford University Press

Oxford   New York   Toronto

Oxford University Press, Walton Street, Oxford OX2 6DP

Oxford New York Toronto
Delhi Bombay Calcutta Madras Karachi
Petaling Jaya Singapore Hong Kong Tokyo
Nairobi Dar es Salaam Cape Town
Melbourne Auckland

and associated companies in
Berlin Ibadan

Oxford is a trade mark of Oxford University Press

Text © Barrie Wade 1991
Illustrations © Irene Wise 1991

First published 1991

Library of Congress Catalog Card Number: 90–050875

British Library Cataloguing in Publication Data
A record of the CIP data is available from the British Library

ISBN 0 19 276091 2

Typeset by Pentacor PLC
Printed and bound in Great Britain by
Butler & Tanner Ltd, Frome and London

for Maggie

Contents

Lies

Lies vanish metro-tunnelled
leaving air still jangled bright as neon.

My mouth stays silted as a found seashell,
its edges rimmed with salt.

My throat's a dried and mossy-sided well
into which no bucket drops.

Truth inside my head still rings —
its crystal goblet struck by fingernails.

Studup

'Owaryer?'
'Imokay.'
'Gladtwearit.'
'Howbowchew?'
'Reelygrate.'
'Binwaytinlong?'
'Longinuff.'
'Owlongubinear?'
'Boutanour.'
'Thinkeelturnup?'
'Aventaclue.'
'Dewfancyim?'
'Sortalykim.'
'Wantadrinkorsummat?'
'Thanksilestayabit.'
'Soocherself.'
'Seeyalater.'
'Byfernow.'

Not wagging but towning

My new school calls it 'towning' or else 'playing hookey'
but really it's the same as 'skiving off' or 'wagging school'

except I've found it's less like puppies on the loose
than stray old dogs with tails hung down

slinking shamefaced down lonely streets
and miserable with nowhere safe to go.

I know there's not a single welcome mat
in brick and concrete and these frozen faces.

I hate this town now more than boys who tease
and teachers who don't seem to care or even see

that all I want is to be let to play
and run along with other folk around

not cold and pushed out to the utmost fringe
like some unwanted mongrel booted down a yard.

School bus

The engine shakes it like a rat.
Icy steel on seatbacks trembles.

Windows shake. Cold and the quiver
chatter teeth. We sit stacked inside

like cards in library catalogues.
The judder thumbs our rows.

We slant and then are left untouched,
inside our breath-fogged capsule,

to dream the spaceship way to school.
Familiar Earth drops spinning in our wake

and minds have fixed upon the day's unknown,
their skills and knowledge rapidly becoming weightless.

Letter to a teacher

Dear Sir, we've had the 'big surprise'
of Secondary. I realize
why you called it that — we're better
off prepared. I hope this letter,

Sir, will not sound too dejected,
for things are much as I expected:
being a minnow in a massive pool
is worlds away from junior school.

It's true that I was apprehensive
of coming to the comprehensive,
when everybody said that it was true
the first-years had their heads pushed down the loo.

Now I know it was a tale invented
to drive the little ones demented;
so reassure them, Sir. They'll lie awake
with worry, if you don't. Try to make

them see it as a cruel fiction.
The only problem here is staff detention —
now they've decided not to use the stick —
and that's no cause to make them worried sick.

I've worked out why you made us finish
cabbage at school lunch. The practice
came in useful: at our cafeteria
now we gobble cooking that's inferior.

If I were you, I'd stop that group work, Sir,
and push the desks back into rows. Up here
there isn't time for talk. There's such a fuss
about not finishing the syllabus.

They make us do a pile of work at home
just as you said. Our teachers spend their time
marking, so they've never had the opportunity
to get good at everything, like you in primary.

Our headmaster has nothing much to do
but dress up in a black cloak like a crow.
Of course they never let him teach.
You wouldn't like it here, Sir, very much.

I know eventually I'll like this place
when there are no surprises left to face.
You've helped me brave the unexpected squarely,
so thank you, Sir, from yours sincerely.

The explanation

From my thicket's safe twilight
I have emerged timorously
seeking an explanation
for multiplying fractions.
This is the third time
my teacher has explained —
once to the class,
twice to me alone.
Each time I see the figures
not the links between them:
random clouds glimpsed
through bracken fronds.
Only this time
I have learned to nod
when his voice rises
and his hand lies still.
. . . *and then you cancel*
this one. Do you see?
I nod. I see,
but do not understand.

$$\frac{3}{14} \times \frac{7}{15} =$$

The pencil moves again.
I watch the fingers
backed with furzy hair
flex and move and stop.
Do you understand it now?
I nod as instinct
draws me back brainfrozen
into tangled bush.
After this explanation
I understand the flash
of fear, the white
glare of failure.
In class I will
copy answers,
learn to look wise,
keep my hand down,
lie doggo in the undergrowth.

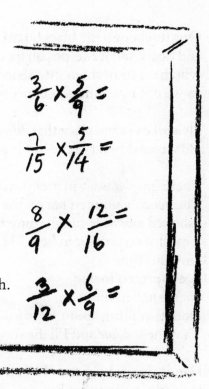

$$\frac{3}{6} \times \frac{5}{9} =$$

$$\frac{7}{15} \times \frac{5}{14} =$$

$$\frac{8}{9} \times \frac{12}{16} =$$

$$\frac{3}{12} \times \frac{6}{9} =$$

Bored work

Our teacher on the blackboard writes twelve words
and dusty silence settles on us yobs
who have to fit them into sentences
so we can learn and so get proper jobs.

He's all over the place that *diligent*.
He wrote down twelve but it was *tenement*.

There once was a squatter in *persistent*.
The *nomad* a pointed hat on his head.
I shoved *minute* in his sleeping bag.
'I can't stand *distinct* in here,' he said.

I get a *potato* clock.
Idolize in bed till noon.
Does that mean about *meander*
That she'll *dilate* and I'll die soon.

Hands that *judicious* can be soft as your face.
It's really no wonder I'm sick of *displace*.

Coming late

Isabel comes late to school.
Tight as a bud in winter
into herself she curls
when our teacher reprimands her.

You are a slack and lazy girl.
You won't be any good . . .
(The voice has risen to a howl
of wind above a frozen wood)

. . . until you learn to come on time
and take more pride and show you care.
Isabel hides a living pain
beneath her blank and frosted stare.

She cannot say her dad has gone,
her mum is ill, she has to dress
and feed her brothers, copes alone
without complaint; will not confess

her courage in a shrivelled life,
will not admit to anyone
that deep inside her is a fragile leaf
craving some warmth to open into sun.

Progress

We're in the progress group, which means we get on slower
than the rest. Nobody calls us 'thick'
or 'dumbo'. Really it's all right in here

and I suppose that it protects us
from exams, and other things that we're no good at.
No one could treat us any better.

We have all attention that we want
and we can misbehave and dream
our days away — for that's expected.

We don't have homework here or marks
put in our books. Red ink would harm us,
shake our charts of progress empty of their stars.

Our world is self-contained, withdrawn into a room
where neither art nor music comes to deflect
our main attack on words and shifting figures.

Science would baffle, so it's left at bay
by handwriting and reading tests
that are the key to proper jobs.

I know we're poor at reading, but
I think I understand the reason why
they don't want any books brought in our room:

we've got to finish all those trays of little cards
and all the questions on them;
we can't be ready for a book just yet.

I've hardly bothered with my tables
since Dad bought me a calculator,
but here they've got us back on coloured rods

and worksheets that have half the answer
there already — we only have to put the figures in
the blanks. I use my calculator. No one minds.

Since I came here, my school report's been good.
It always says I'm 'trying hard'
and 'overcoming problems only gradually'.

I think that means I shouldn't use the calculator,
but at least it doesn't say I'm 'messy'
or 'lacking concentration', as it did before.

Now 'working well within his limitations'
is what *I* am, so I don't mind
being limited to this one room

and missing out on music, fun and poetry.
Drama and stories I'll soon learn to do without
— all in the name of progress, you understand.

20 *Barley Barley*

The writer

She is the one who sits and thinks.
When Miss says *write* our pens race into gear,
twist through letter loops and word chicanes
with minds tight-bunched and hammering to overtake.
It is as if in pole position she has stalled.
Her brow is radiator furrowed.
She judders at her desk
and I can see that Miss is trying not
to lean across to give a push.
By the lesson's end her littered page
shows fragments of tyretread
patterned into asphalt
and yet

She is the one who stands and reads
next day while we sit breathless,
whose words splash coloured images
brilliant as petrol spilled in puddles
that we passed along our way.

Revised version

Come ye blank-faced singers, come,
Raise the song of harvest home.
All be safely gathered in,
Ere resit exams begin.
Scattered facts are gathered in,
Jumbled, mumbled through the hymn.
Ripe and swollen are our brains,
Crammed like silos packed with grains.

Glancing round, I see some eyes
Lifted hopeless to the skies,
Sure their Maker won't provide
For their wants to be supplied.
On the shifting sand of doubt
They have lived their schooldays out;
And the best amongst us found
Teaching fall on stony ground.

Wheat and tares together sown
Unto joy or sorrow grown;
Fruits of mixed ability,
Soon to reach their destiny.
Some are doomed to find their place:
Further failure, more disgrace.
Grant, O harvest Lord, that we
This time pass G.C.S.E.

School photograph

No need to call for quiet in assembly. Death
beneath its camera-cloth had posed us
motionless — without a thought of running round
to pose again. While the news swept over us, breath
lay hushed in mouths — much like his, I supposed — as
well-polished words lent his image sharper background.

Those snapshot phrases I remember still. The Head's
grey tones: *. . . an accident . . . unfortunate sad loss
. . . remember with affection.* Later, playground spite
grew callous: *. . . take a book to Physics . . . Camera Club's
been cancelled . . . wish I hadn't done his homework.* No gloss
from temporary grief could cover how he wasn't liked.

Later still, when headlines blew him larger than death
or life had done (TEACHER SLAIN BY JEALOUS HUSBAND,
SECRET STUDIO SHOOTING, 'MODEL' WIFE HEART-BROKEN),
we added tints of pride that glorified the truth
and framed him with his film wound on, his shutter jammed,
his mouth an aperture set permanently open.

Retiring

I gave to your collection, Sir,
and I understand they've bought
an easel and a box of oils
and squirrel brushes in each size.

I picture you in shirtsleeves
measuring your Cotswolds with a thumb,
the way you taught us, and your brush
poised like a baton to conduct.

Colour always was your element. I learned
the thrill of cobalt stroked with red —
'Kingfishers flashed with fire,' you said —
and how all shadows are not black.

No matter how you pushed them up
your shirtsleeves always flapped in paint.
You hung your paintings amongst ours
to dry upon the floor at dinnertime.

Kitchen ladies clucked at paint-crammed
fingernails that worked like silent
talismans between us, crescents
varnishing our gloss of pride.

Since leaving Secondary myself
I rarely get it in my nails.
In our job mostly we use rollers.
Brushwork isn't wanted, only speed;

and yet I'd like you at my side
to see a special finished gloss
or when I've toned a colour down
with yellow and it comes just right.

I do a lot of factory walls in grey
and office blocks magnolia room by room.
All these make empty canvasses
to fill with pictures from my mind.

I see you at your leaving party
with your blue-washed eyes gone cloudy
like the little jars of water
that we used to rinse our brushes in.

Behind bars

Sent back to search for my lost coat,
I shudder in the wintry
evening chill outside locked gates,

grip smooth, cold bars, a prisoner
returning late from his parole,
hope going out with light.

Silence has turned its deadlock round
our school, mist blurs the branches
of our single playground oak

and cramp of iron pains my hands.
Across the chalk of dying sky
starlings in their smoke-plume drift,

billow and fragment. Their black
blizzard scribbles pages over
darkened roof tops. Their excited

chatter shrills. They shake like pepper
on the tree: its branches over-
spill with wingbeats. Come alive,

the playground swells with squabble.
Spaces between bars and brickwork
fill with clattered mugs and plates on steel
needing night's final warning bell.

Our music

Like armchairs under dustsheets in locked rooms
adults sit veiled and still beneath smoke skeins,
while lights submerge us in a sea of greens
and blues and reds. Our disco music booms
and its insistent strobe splashes our jeans
while we pulsate where no large shadow looms
to dim our colours or turn down our tunes.
Our fluent limbs express what freedom means.

Invasion of our space is not a threat:
we tolerate the ones who try our style,
jerking like broken puppets out of time.
Our music makes them inarticulate,
gawky and graceless, gauche and juvenile.
Discreetly we enjoy their pantomime.

Don't

Don't comb your hair in company.
Don't cross the kitchen floor in welly boots.
Don't put the television on.
Don't squint. Don't get in fights.

Don't stuff your mouth with sausage.
Don't drop towels on the bathroom floor.
Don't hang about with that rough crowd.
Don't put your feet up on the chair.

Don't use up all the paper in the loo.
Don't scratch. Don't twitch. Don't sniff. Don't talk.
Don't stick your tongue out.
Don't you dare to answer back.

Life is full of opportunity, says my Mum.

Cotoneasters

They tell us, 'Live your life non-stop.
Responsibilities will come
to stunt your spread, to dull your gloss
and drain your lifeblood drop by drop.'

Cotoneaster shrubs — their first, cream
childlike flowering long past —
yawn in our borders, while their fruit
sets scarlet on to lingering green.

Their blood-drop berries soon attract
turmoils of early-winter birds
that dip the boughs with haste
and worry. Gold-rimmed greed unchecked

shows in the blackbird's brazen wink;
the throstle's pulsing throat is filled;
all crimson fades to blood smears
on a cream-browed redwing's flank.

We shall endure the adulthood
of winter, feel our loves stripped off;
but now we wait, sharpening our thorns.
In time we also will draw blood.

Rabbits

Docile, tamed
the rabbit sits in straw
chewing, chewing
in a hutch
no bigger than a box.

At night its hindlegs thump alarms
inside their wooden drum
and warning flash of white
unseen is swallowed by the gloom.

Curtain-close
on our estate shuts in
other silent figures
hunched in rooms
where lakes of colour spill.

The boxes that contain them,
with their past and present joys
and all their future hopes, flash
and resound with light and noise.

Teenagers

In the days before backgardens
winter muffled minds with snow.
Our backyards trapped it drifted, soft
like mousse before it hardens.

There always was enough
to build huge snowmen
that lingered on to shrink
after we'd sickened of the stuff.

Now we long for silent snow
to smother hurt, blur insight's edge;
but all uncomplicated joys
melted several years ago.

Now our lawns have criss-cross scars
where we've scraped snowballs
up to sling against the fence
in spite of passage of our years.

On bitter days too cold for snow
silent, armless ranks of snowmen
fill our memories of childhood.
Bland faces say, 'We told you so.'

Answering back

'Don't you dare to answer back,' she bawls.
Eyes go blank and fixed ahead
unseeing like a soldier's on parade.

'Stop looking insolent,' she yells.
Lips have bladed like a dagger
and my finger tightens on a trigger.

'Go up to your room!' Her screaming shrills.
Feet have scrambled up the dugout steps
and jellied legs don't feel the barbed wire rips.

Now anger bursts its shrapnel shells
inside my heart is time for no regrets
and all my kindest thoughts are turned to bayonets.

Work experience

Come from her orchard
Aunty Mary brings her wholesome smell
of apples newly picked, showered in rain,
wind-dried, fruity fresh.
Her blotchy windfall hands lie still.
Nervous as blackbirds,
her eyes peck and then take flight.

Uncle Dennis works in pig sheds
whose lively stink sinks in his skin,
clings at his clothing fibres.
His nostrils permanently wrinkle
and his voice is guttural as if
imagined clothes-pegs held his nose.
His hands swing in air like hams.

While at their place
I give them both a hand —
though carefully.

Our Dad

dances to music in the wine shop,
will argue after drinking beer,
wants to hold hands in the street,
scoots on supermarket trolleys,
sings Christmas carols out of tune,
shows old photos of us to our friends,
tells us off for watching television,
watches darts and snooker half the night,
falls fast asleep in chairs,
leans his elbows on the table,
never sits up straight,
wears clothes a clown would soon discard,
will not talk quietly in shops,
tells the same old sausage joke,
laughs before the end of it,
burps deliberately, then pretends it's me.

Our Grandma had a hard life.

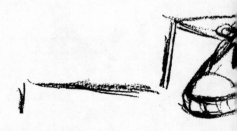

Ironing

Sinews flexed like rooted briars,
hair slicked by fluorescent light,
my father at the ironing board,

arm balanced as his single skate
slides over dampened cloth — the hiss
and puff of steam like icedust

rising over bladed creases —
and his gaze goes down a life's canal
past blizzards to his midnight jaunts

on ribboned, frozen water
with the studded pit-boots deftly
smoothing creases out of ice.

Museums

I've watched my father set like ancient stone.
Since the time his factory closed two years ago
his eyes have fixed behind their bone
like marble carved by Michelangelo.

Writing off for jobs he'll spend an age
staring ahead. He tenses as he writes,
displays against the neat, half-written page
those redundant fingers stiff as ammonites.

It's then our house goes quiet as the places
where he used to take me on wet Saturdays
and we sit separate as showcases
kept locked in high and endless galleries.

I remember how blind statues stand
like hope run cold against a dark tomorrow.
It's then I long to hold him by the hand
as he held mine what seems an age ago.

Out to service

Frail as the lace she wore at wrist and throat,
my Great-Gran used to tell me how she started out
at just fourteen to work for well-to-dos.

I still know all their names: Albert, Sarah,
Arthur, Reginald, Emma and Clara,
especially the little ones who died.

I was 'just like Edward' when I wouldn't touch
the porridge. 'Poor Emily' had 'just my eyes'
and long-dead William shared 'my winning ways'.

I shared their illnesses and sad goodbyes:
their brass and polished wood for leaving home,
the gleaming silver in a darkened room.

They never let me see *her* when *she* died
and yet imagination was enough
to picture filigree collar and cuff,

arranged like doilies on her velvet dress;
and how she settled down to her last rest
with all the creases ironed from her face;

and how she went again to service dressed
more well-to-do than all the rest.
My Great-Gran always said she knew her place.

Parents

They share a bathroom and a bed,
buy each other dressing-gowns
and only kiss in greeting.
Their days are spent apart:
variations to the metronomic
tune that keeps them going,
now that time has shifted
impulse to a habit.
She has stopped her music lessons.
He has lost interest in clocks.
Invariably they watch the late TV,
too tired to go early to bed.
Waking, I hear their tread
and then their light clicks off.
My closed-up room
holds its chord as if a piano
played inside has stopped.

Desert island

A schoolboy and his father sit
islanded and opposite.
Their kitchen table's harsh formica
tilts the glare to drill behind glazed eyes.

Hands lie beached on homework book and magazine.
Dishes are neatly stacked to drain.
Eyes have foundered in the central blur,
avoiding any contact with each other.

The mother by her absence
is made more sharply present.
Brash seas of cold formica mirage
hazed lagoons from which she beckons

dolphin-like and gentle-eyed
or ample breasted as a figurehead,
hopeful, yearning, shearing ocean emptiness
until such images dissolve to strands of kelp

and lightwashed eyes go pale as mist
dazed by long looking down a wave-rocked past.
Captain and shipboy still survive marooned
but vaguely troubled still by thoughts of home.

Sunday visiting

On Sunday mornings I leave home
to spend my one fixed day with Dad.
My Mum won't ever say his name
as if she thinks of him as dead.

Sunday visiting she calls it.
Tightlipped as a tombstone she goes
herself to see our Gran whose grave
is just inside the churchyard gate.

The stairs above the butcher's shop I climb
for my 'unreasonable access'. Dad
calls it that, though every smile fades on his lips
and all his ancient jokes are growing sad.

His place is musty, smells of earth
that's newly dug, and on his wall
these sooty toadstools sometimes grow.
Dad says he's back to nature now.

I wait till Dad is stretched asleep
after his dinner and the beer,
then by the flickering TV light
I scrape down every fungoid sphere.

Their stench is foul, unbearable
like breath of ghouls returned from earth
to say that life is meaningless
and all is pain and death and loss.

Rooted in damp they will return
like moss or lichen scraped from stone,
but on our Sunday visitings
we must keep busy. Life goes on.

Kites

You had a way with newspaper and sticks.
Your diamond framework never snapped. Your sheets
of paper, painted red, would never tear.

Once you had strung the tail with newsprint bows
it was as if you had command of air,
your hurled-high kite the go-between on twine;

so it is hard to visualize your smash
on ordinary rocks that show no sign
of blood or red hang-glider antics,

much less the mystery of why you stalled,
whether you hung an instant crucifixed,
saw your framework sag, felt rocks jag and beckon

as though reeling you back down. My body
flinches from the memory of sudden
dips, erratic loops, the shadow racing

over grass and that last steep sickening
plunge, the shadow gone, torn air returning
and every trace of soaring disappeared.

Canal

They started sending
coal by railway.
By my childhood
it was in advanced

decay, its barges gone,
its waters choked,
but still its cinder
towpath led us

over orchard walls
or down to stinking
silted pools in which
we steeped bare-legged

to let its leeches come.
We peeled them off
in matchboxes —
severed finger-ends

to scare our mothers.
Sticklebacks we swung
in string-handled jars
as emblems of our pride.

We carted bucket-loads
of spawn away,
yet still its teeming
banks and waters croaked.

The miners fished
for roach and eels
in deeper sections
where they cut reeds down.

We owned its shallow
pools and root-clogged swamps,
its jungles fertile
with incident

where bullrushes made
spears and arrow reeds
stopped tigers in their tracks.
The sticky sweetness

followed us home
comforting as
water squelching warm
inside our boots.

Now they have filled
the gaps in which
imagination
showed its silver fin.

Our stretch lies buried
under private housing
and on summer
afternoons a few

old miners squat
at dry street corners.
Their eyes swivel froglike
after passing cars.

Haiku calendar: Southern version
(for Ken Watson)

In the sun's oven
New Year bakes to perfection
iced by the ocean.

February nights
with softness you can touch
like possums in gumtrees.

March dries orange leaves
on gnarled, blackened trunks after
the bushfire summer.

Like a kangaroo
this April afternoon lies
stretched in the cool dust.

From cold May mornings
the warmth of Autumn soars in
canopies of blue.

Like an owl's feather
the year's first snowflake settles
into dusky June.

July holds its breath
in silent valleys muffled
by the drifted snow.

Cloud-splitting August
flashes silver rivers down
sky's thunder mountains.

After winter rain
September like an emu
treads so warily.

October sunset:
a wedge of black cockatoos
calls wheel-oo wheel-oo.

November sunrise
feathers greying sky with pink:
galahs on the move.

Flaming December:
sulphur-crested cockatoos
dip the year in gold.

Haiku calendar: Northern version

Keen January,
frost-bladed at the earth's edge,
slices to the bone.

Bleak February
glares through baleful eyes of rooks
hunched on bare branches.

Torn clouds in the wind
go helter-skelter, pell-mell:
March rushes headlong.

Songthrush April sings
again again again its
rhapsody for Spring.

May gives its promise
with apple trees unfurling
petal flags of peace.

In egg-warming June
the nightingale's throat is still;
even leaves relax.

Simmering July:
the lime tree sizzles with bees
and bubbles over.

August stamps its foot,
strikes sparks off towering clouds,
shows its bad temper.

September stringtime:
swallows thread themselves on wires;
dangled conkers spin.

Golden October
mints its coins in plums and pears.
Leaves reflect the fire.

Dreary November:
cherry trees droop skeletal,
shrink into themselves.

December shivers
kaleidoscopic pieces
out of leaden skies.

Palm Sunday

That one day in Jerusalem
a man went riding in
along a welcome path of palms
to celebrate the Passover.

This Saturday in Redditch Centre
shoppers shuttle by
beneath redundant palm leaves
safely out of reach.

That one day hoof and sandal
turned the palm leaves underfoot
to print a welcome message
across two thousand years.

This Saturday no eyes look back
or lift beyond shopwindow height;
and decorative palms
will neither praise them nor condemn.

Today into imagination come
those folded palm leaf crosses
given out in Sunday School.
I pinned them pointing down

the ages back to Calvary.
We should maybe blade them
pointing upwards, poised
to scratch a meaning back to life.

The visitors

'Twenty-seven lamps is what it takes,' he said,
setting his little candles on the stairs,
'to light the way and welcome back the dead.'
I helped him light their little welcome flares

because he's my best mate. His Dad and Mum
were Buddhists and I know his Obon feast
means food set out for visitors to come
seeking *Nirvana* which, he says, is *peace*.

'At Obon we invite them to return
and visit us.' He paused with eyes alight —
like mine, I guess, on Christmas Eve, when wine
is left for Santa Claus. 'They'll come tonight.'

I know his grandad and his mother drowned,
with nearly everybody from their junk,
under the China Seas when bandits rammed
their overcrowded boat. He would have sunk

but for his dad and sister who took turns
to hold him up. I reckon one who's
rescued from a hell like that soon learns
what welcome lights we can't afford to lose.

'We'll burn the paper lantern now,' he said.
'Grandad used to make them out of lotus
leaves, but this will have to do instead.'
I pray and hope it helps them reach us

in these flats. I watch his eyes go still and wide
with peaceful welcome. In the flickering glare
his face is like a beacon lit to guide
the old man and his daughter up the stair.

Shortcut

The moon slides down
on its silver skate,
buffs the ribboned water
like a rifle barrel
rigid in a velvet case.

Leaving the towpath
to cross the graveyard,
you duck through hawthorns,
soaked and black, their twigs
unyielding as wire.

Rotted in their jars,
chrysanthemums
spread a stench upwards:
like sickness in the throat
it climbs unstoppable

except by winter frost
that cracks the little jars,
subdues the slime on stalks,
and stifles every flower mouth
with frozen hands of ice.

The asphalt leads on past
that row of child-sized graves
whose grey stones, floating
in the moonlight, mark
where children lie below.

The canal split
and they together
plunged to darkness
under sealing ice.
They made a dumbshow

for their final act:
under the moon's floodlighting
trapped and twisted mouths
mimed earth's relentless
suffocating grip.

Wetted ice shone like
the churchyard's newdug clay,
each spadeful stealing
from the digger's blade
some temporary gloss.

Their lives were cut
short as these graves.

The thought's enough
to make you hold a gun
to Winter's head and seek

to pass directly on
to Spring's sweet mowing heaps,
to blossoms in the hedge
and, on a tensioned surface,
to waterboatmen scudding safe.

Night machine

TILT
went the sky
and the moonball
clattered down
silver and
rolling and
lighting and
flashing and
bouncing off clouds.

Under the housetops
it dropped.

GAME OVER.

Paperboy

Half-past six and I'm awake,
listening for his creaky bike
and for the crunch his footsteps make
along the path to our front door.

The creaking stops when he jumps off,
then vaults our fence and strides our path.
I know his whistle, sniff and cough
and every day I love him more.

But I am secret as a fox
with pounding heart. I steal no looks
until our clattered letterbox
signals it's safe to cross the floor,

to shift the curtains just a trace,
to glimpse retreating paradise.
He never turns that lovely face,
but every day I love him more.

At school he never looks my way
and if he spoke to me I'd die.
My feelings are not for display:
they are too new, too strange, too raw.

I know love comes and walks away
as careless as our paperboy,
but in the early blush of day
my love for love grows more and more.

Destinations

Morning and our bathroom mirror marks
departure point.
Eyes meet briefly, flicker, startle off,
nervous fauns disturbed,
so my reflection can transact
its known routines —
a busied booking clerk safely framed
behind a screen.

Around me in unhurried certainty pass
punctual feet;
suitcases stop their pendulums flexed
on steady arms;
restrained like kites, young children fly strung
at arm's length,
their faces closed and eyes already
at a distance.

I seem to be the anxious one that scans
the flickering boards
for certainty so I at least might
be *approaching,*
if *not yet due to arrive,* alarmed
that I might
terminate at Birmingham without
a change at Crewe
or even *calling at Watford Junction*
and the face
behind the glass won't tell me where,
or if, I'm going.

First death

Catching light above the estuary
wailing flocks of waders tilt
and shake their aluminium foil.

His arm is flung above his head
with the gesture that sunbathers use;
likewise his posture, loose.
Strewn on to the tideline, he rests
with stranded weed and broken shells.

Too much sun, I thought at first,
seeing the water-bloated, purple skin
and bloom of salt hazing that face,
plum-ripe for its own bursting,
the lips drawn back to a smile.

The shore birds wheeled again.
Skylids above the rivermouth
closed upon the end of childhood.

Wolf in the park

Upon unfeeling paws he treads
a never-ceasing rampage;
his repetitions wear a path
inside the wire of his cage.

An age ago men hunted down
the last wild British wolves.
They tracked the cubs to dismal caves
and killed them all with clubs.

This one they fetched from Arctic wastes,
a crated, snarling beast,
to remind us of that wildness
which lived here ages past.

Not once has he been heard to howl
his menace or his miseries,
for even anger has been hammered
from his glazed, unseeing eyes.

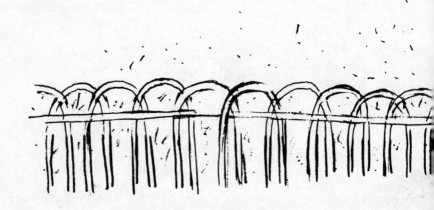

The sun beats on his tangled coat,
takes light out of his eyes.
He paces still a wilderness,
still stares at leaden skies.

His thoughts are in a frozen waste.
His heart is ice and stone.
Captivity has clubbed his brain,
set madness in his bone

and locked him on this single track
he treads with insane fervour.
He cannot bring that wildness back.
His winter lasts forever.

Park

Our gang pass its locked gates
en route for Friday discos.
Sometimes we rattle railings;
sometimes we pass mute,
our heads like padlocks looped in chains.

Then, if we peer inside,
the slide is lurching at the moon,
the see-saw totters sideways,
swings dangle drunken
and, on the concrete,
broken bottles wink and leer.

Our feet scuff on the road outside.
Now leaves no longer sing for us,
we have begun to understand our history.
It is not to us that flowers speak:
our childhoods all are safely locked away.

Barley Barley

It always was our den:
place of crossed fingers, truce
and claims for sanctuary.

Our hands stroked its ridges
smooth. It endured kicks, blades
and climbs without complaint.

Its leafsheath grasped at sunshine
from a blindfold, fluted
winds played hide and seek down

sprawling boughs and sparrows
chased among its acorns
in tag and kiss-catch games.

It thickened underneath:
roots buckling their dragon
coils crumbled the asphalt,

swelled against the brickwork.
One January day,
miserable with loss,

we watched its branches bonfired
or carted off in logs,
felt the old trunk topple

like the end of childhood,
heard the scream of saw-teeth
bite with all our future pain.

Thoughtfully they have shaped
the stump into a seat
where we can choose to sit

listening to remembered
voices of our youth filling
the gap and emptiness of air:

Barley! Barley! One, two, three!